LAUGHABLE
LATIN

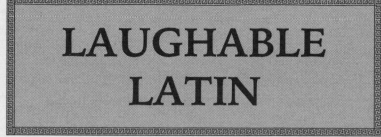

LAUGHABLE LATIN

WITTY LATIN PHRASES
FOR ALL OCCASIONS

Compiled by
Lesley O'Mara

Translated by
Rose Williams

Michael O'Mara Humour

Published in Great Britain in 2004 by
Michael O'Mara Books Limited
9 Lion Yard, Tremadoc Road
London SW4 7NQ

Previously published in paperback in 1999 as *Veni Vidi Vici*
by Michael O'Mara Books Limited

A CIP catalogue record for this book is available from the
British Library

ISBN 1-84317-097-3

1 3 5 7 9 10 8 6 4 2

Lesley O'Mara is the Managing Director of Michael O'Mara Books,
as well as the editor of numerous anthologies of short stories.
The compilation of *Laughable Latin* was inspired by her love of
language, travel and history.

Rose Williams has been a scholar of Latin since her college days in
Waco, Texas, attending numerous universities in the US and, more
recently, studying medieval Latin literature in England and Italy.
Professionally, Rose has taught Latin at high school and university
level, and given numerous lectures, seminars and workshops for
various societies and museums in America. Also an author of several
Latin teaching guides, Rose Williams is unquestionably an expert in
her field, and a true devotee of the Latin language.

Designed and typeset by K DESIGN

Printed and bound in Great Britain by Cox & Wyman, Reading, Berks

◆ CONTENTS ◆

PLANNING
◆ AHEAD ◆

**Have they had any barbarians around
there lately?**
Barbarosne ibi nuper habuerunt?

◆

**I'd like to ask the soothsayer if I should
go to the North or the South.**
*Utrum debeam ire ad septentriones an meridiem
augurem rogare cupio.*

◆

How many gods do they have there?
Quot deos ibi habent?

◆

When did the ship last come in?
Quando venit ultima navis?

◆

Can I rent a slave there?
Servumne ibi conducere possum?

◆

I need tickets for me and my fourteen servants.
Tesseris mihi et quattuordecim servis egeo.

◆

Let's not go to the Bay of Naples again.
All the plebs go there.
Ne eamus ad Sinum Neapolis iterum. Plebs ibi it.

◆

Can you interpret this sign from the gods?
Hoc signum e deis interpretare potes?

◆

I need to find a moneylender.
Faenatorem invenire opus est mihi.

◆

You're not getting me into a boat that small!
In scapham tam parvam me non ducis!

◆

III

I think we should go on a grand tour
of the Empire.

Puto in itinere magno Imperii ire nos debere.

We can't go tomorrow; the sacred chickens
aren't eating.

Cras non poterimus ire; pulli sacri non edunt.

We should avoid the road they use for the
lions and tigers.

Viam qua cum leonibus et tigribus utuntur vitemus.

Is there a road between those towns?
I couldn't stand another boat journey.

*Estne via inter oppida illa? Non iter aliud in
scapha ferre possum.*

Where did Antony and Cleopatra go this year?
Ubi Antonius et Cleopatra hoc anno ibant?

◆

I need to take a lot of writing paper; the trip is going to last for five days.
Cartam multam capere egeo;
iter quinque dies durabit.

Apparently, if you sit on one of those leaves you'll survive the journey.
Evidenter si sedes in uno foliorum
illorum itineri superes.

Can I rent a litter?
Possum conducere lecticam?

That slave doesn't look strong enough to carry me.
Servus ille fortis satis portare me non apparet.

I think I'll have to buy my own galley next time.
Puto me actuariam meam emere proxime debere.

I need a good strong tent. There are no hotels in that town.
Egeo tabernaculo fortissimo. Sunt non cauponae in illo oppido.

Is it nice and hot at this time of year?
Estne caelum iucunde calidum hoc tempore anni?

I don't think much of your charioteering skills.
Non artem currus tuam amo.

That was a very bumpy ride.
Erat vectum asperrimum.

Are we nearly there yet?
Paene advenimus?

Don't say you forgot to bring a spare wheel.
Noli dicere te rotam aliam ferre oblitum esse.

◆

I fancy the Greek islands this summer.
Insulas Graecas hoc aestate videre desidero.

◆

Should it take this long to cross the Channel?
Transire Canalem tantum tempus eget?

Who was in this litter?
Look at the state of it.
Quis erat in lectica hac?
Specta statum eius.

How far will we get in four weeks and two days?
Quatenus in hebdomades quattuor et dies duos ire possumus?

◆

I'll do the navigating from now on.
In posterum navigabo.

◆

Do you have anything for seasickness?
Habesne medicamentum nauseae?

◆

Do all roads lead to Rome?
Viaene omnes vere Romam ducunt?

◆

Can I borrow your chariot, my friend?
Currum tuum, amice mi, mutuari possum?

◆

◆ SIGHTSEEING ◆

Not another feast day!
Non aliud festum!

◆

Where can I hire a litter?
Ubi lecticam conducere possum?

◆

Where is the chariot racetrack?
Ubi est circus?

◆

Is my chariot big enough?
Habetne currus meus magnitudinis satis?

◆

It's a shame that statue has lost his arm.
Imago bracchium amisit – triste est.

◆

Take me to the soothsayer.
Duc me ad augurem.

◆

Have I missed the news in the forum?
Amisine rumores in foro?

◆

Where can I buy a statue of Hadrian to take home?

Ubi imaginem Hadriani quam domum portem emere possum?

◆

Haven't you got a temple yet in this town?

Num habes templum in hoc oppido etiamnunc?

◆

Slave, carry me over to get a better look at that statue.

Serve, porta me ut melius illam imaginem spectem.

◆

Don't the locals make anything worth buying as a souvenir?

Nonne indigenae aliquid dignum emendi faciunt?

◆

Where's the action in this place?
Ubi est actio hic?

◆

This building is very grand.
Hoc aedificium magnificentissimum est.

Did Caesar use to live here?
Habitabatne Caesar hic?

◆

I don't think much of this amphitheatre.
Hoc amphitheatrum non amo.

◆

We've got a much bigger marketplace at home.
Forum maius multo domi habemus.

◆

Doesn't anyone speak proper Latin around here?
Nonne quisquis hic Latine decenter loquitur?

◆

I lost all my money at the races.
Pecuniam totam meam in cursibus amisi.

◆

What a wonderful pair of knockers!
Mirabile par percussionum!

◆

I've never seen so many bars.
Numquam tot tabernas vidi.

◆

**Where's the nearest sundial? I need to
know the time.**
Ubi est horologium proximum? Opus est mihi scire horam.

◆

This is just a one-horse town.
Oppidum equi unius hoc est.

◆

There's a nice bit of booty in that temple.
Est praeda dulcis in illo templo.

◆

Any good orgies here this week?
Orgia bona hic in his septem diebus?

◆

Beware of the dog.
Cave canem.

Why is that man running through the street without a toga?
Cur ille sine toga per viam currit?

AT THE
◆ HOTEL ◆

Aren't these the servants' rooms?
Nonne sunt hae camerae servorum?

◆

What, no running water?
Quid, non aqua currens?

◆

You need some more urine on that cloth.
In lino illo plus ureae eges.

◆

Just look at the sewage on that pavement.
Specta sentinam in pavimento.

◆

You don't have enough slaves in this hotel.
Non satis servorum in hac caupona habes.

◆

Go and cut down some trees.
It's cold in here.
I et secta arbores quasdam. Frigidum hic est.

◆

The room service is very poor.
Ministerium camerae pessimum est.

◆

How often are these rooms cleaned?
They're full of dust.
Quoties hae camerae purgatae sunt? Pulverulentissimae sunt.

◆

This bedding is too hard.
Durissima haec stragula est.

◆

Isn't there a sauna in here?
Non est sudatorium hic?

This decor is not very tasteful.
Hoc ornamentum non decorum est.

◆

I need a maid . . . now!
Famula egeo . . . nunc!

◆

This is the worst hotel I've ever stayed in.
Caupona pessima in qua mansi haec est.

◆

I demand to speak to the manager.
Postulo dicere cum administratore.

◆

Is dinner included?
Cenane includitur?

◆

I'll meet you in the foyer.
In vestibulo tibi occurram.

◆

Our room is very stuffy.
Camera nostra clausissima est.

Damned mosquitoes!
Damnati mosquitoes!

I can hear him snoring next door.
Eius rhoncum in camera proxima audire possum.

◆

Has the fan stopped working?
Ventilumne laborare desivit?

◆

I wish our room didn't overlook the main street.
It's so noisy.
Utinam camera nostra super viam principalem non esset.
Clamosissima est.

◆

Where's the chamber pot kept?
Ubi est olla camerae?

◆

Come up and see my frescos.
Veni et vide picturas meas.

◆

AT THE PUBLIC
◆ BATHS ◆

Are you here to cure a disease?
Venistine ut morbum sanes?

◆

Go and get me my strigil.
I et fer mihi strigilem meam.

◆

That hot air up your toga feels good, doesn't it?
Nonne aura calida in togam est bona?

◆

Hey! That's my toga!
Heus! Illa est mea toga!

◆

Are your scabs better yet?
Suntne scabies tuae meliores?

◆

Pass me a book roll would you?
Da mihi volumen, sis?

◆

**No, it's not from the library; it's from
my private collection.**
Non est e bibliotheca; est ex libris meis.

◆

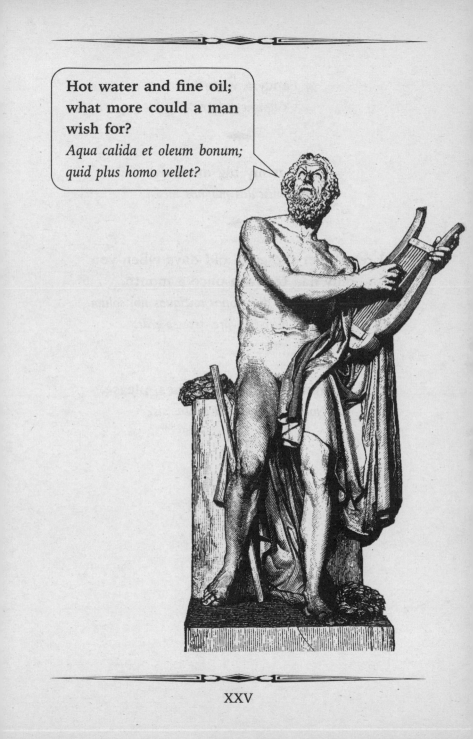

Hot water and fine oil;
what more could a man
wish for?

Aqua calida et oleum bonum;
quid plus homo vellet?

Fancy a wrestle?
Cupisne luctari?

Look at my big muscles!
Specta musculos magnos meos!

I remember the good old days when you only had to wash once a month.
Habeo in memoria dies bonos antiquos ubi solum semel in mense lavare necesse erat.

Don't make such big splashes, please.
Noli facere aspersa tanta, sis.

**You can see the women were in here
this morning.**
Potes videre feminas adfuisse mane.

◆

Where's that boy with the cakes?
Ubi est puer cum dulcibus?

◆

I'm an invalid; I need it extra hot.
Sum infirmus; egeo aqua calidissima.

◆

This marble is a bit slippery.
Marmor est lubricum.

◆

Can only one person sing in the
bath at once, please?
Licetne uno solo in balneo canere, sivis?

Call me old-fashioned, but I think 2,000 at
once is plenty, otherwise it's a bit too crowded.
*Voca me obsoletum, sed puto duo milia simul
esse satis, aliter confertissimum esse.*

It's a shame they won't let
women in at the same time,
don't you think?
*Nonne est turpe mulieres
simul non admitti?*

◆

He's sulking because his
wife tried to murder him
this morning.
*Morosus est quod uxor eius eum
necare mane temptavit.*

◆

He had a bad dream last night.
Nocte proxima somnium malum habuit.

You don't mean they let women in every day?
Num significas eos mulieres cotidie admittere?

**Warm up some asses' milk to clean my face,
will you?**
Sivis, cale lac asinorum ad lavandum vultum meum?

Can you paint over my bald patch?
Pingere calvam maculam potes?

How very unsociable he is.
Inimicissimus est.

Can I book a slave for after my sauna?
Postne sudatorium servum conducere possum?

◆

I'd like a nice oil rub.
Desidero fricatum cum oleo.

◆

That tickles!
Ille titallat!

◆

Quiet down there. I'm trying to sleep.
Silete illic. Dormire tempto.

◆

Oh no, the ink's running.
Eheu, atramentum oblinit.

◆

Get back to the women's quarters.
Redi ad cameras mulierum.

◆

I saw a man in the women's changing rooms!
Vidi virum in apodyteriis mulierum!

◆

I don't believe it; my toga's been stolen again.
Hoc non credo; toga mea surrepta est iterum.

◆

Someone's swapped my new toga for this old thing!
Aliquis togam novam meam panno antiquo mutavit!

◆

THE PUBLIC
◆ TOILETS ◆

**I'm going down to the public toilets for
some company.**
Ad latrinas publicas pro societate ibo.

◆

Only a six-seater toilet?
Modo sex sellae in latrina?

◆

Pass the sponge on a stick, please.
Da mihi spongiam in fuste, sis.

Wipe it first.
Primum deterge eam.

◆

This sponge has seen better days.
Haec spongia melior fuit.

◆

Are you still here?
Esne hic etiamnunc?

◆

Have you had that problem for long?
Habebasne onus illud diu?

◆

Is there a fan in here?
Estne ventilum hic?

◆

We have proper bathrooms back home.
Domi latrinas decentes habemus.

◆

It's no fun going to the toilet with you two!
Non jocularia est ire cum duobus vobis ad latrinas!

◆

When was the water last changed?
Ubi aqua mutata est?

◆

Would you like to come to my banquet?
Desideras venire ad convivium meum?

◆

This lavatory is frozen!
Lavatrina haec gelida est!

◆

I don't think you should have eaten all those grapes.
Non puto te debere edisse uvas illas omnes.

◆

I wouldn't step over there if I were you.
Si essem tu, non illic graderer.

◆

There's a nasty draught blowing through here.
Ventus malus per hunc locum flat.

Are there any clean sponge sticks?
Suntne in fuste spongiae castae?

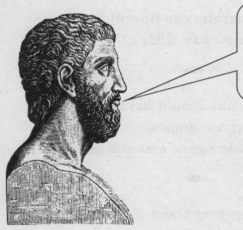

**It's very crowded
in here today.**
*Celebratissimum hic
hodie est.*

**Mind you don't tread in anything
unpleasant!**
Specta ne in laetro gradiaris!

Thanks for the chat. See you again soon!
Gratias pro sermone. Videam te mox!

Please don't watch. It puts me off . . .
Noli spectare. Perturbat me . . .

I've never seen a sixty-seater before!
Numquam antehac sexaginta sellas vidi!

**Whoever dreamed up these places had no
sense of smell.**
*Quicumque loca haec designavit non sensum
odorationis habuit.*

Fancy seeing you here!
Stupui videre te hic!

◆

Oh, you are awful!
O, horrendus es!

◆

I've waited a long time for this.
Diu hoc exspectavi.

◆

Where's my good-luck token?
Ubi est signum meum fortunae?

◆

I prefer the two-seaters myself.
Ipse duas sellas malo.

◆

◆ TO THE ARENA ◆

Things to shout

◆

Thrash him!
Verbera eum!

◆

Kill him!
Neca eum!

◆

Let him go!
Libera eum!

◆

Which way to the execution?
Qua semita ad stragem?

◆

Who's supposed to kill whom?
Quis quem necare debet?

◆

Is he dead yet?
Estne mortuus nunc?

◆

That one's still moving!
Iste movet etiamnunc!

◆

Ooh, look at his big pecs.
O, specta musculos magnos pectoralis.

◆

That gladiator is only fit for lion food.
Ille gladiator est idoneus alendo leonem.

Hey, he's groaning. He's not supposed to groan.
Heus, gemit. Non gemere exspectatus est.

It would be more interesting if he were allowed a shield.
Esset delectantius si scutum haberet.

Why is the Emperor cheering?
Cur Imperator clamat?

I say, it's a bit bloodthirsty, isn't it?
Ecastor, nonne est paululum cruentum?

That one is definitely dead.
Ille certe mortuus est.

I don't think it's very nice to make women fight.
Non puto decorum esse cogere mulieres pugnare.

Is he going to be torn apart by wild animals?
Estne laceraturus a feris?

It gets a bit repetitive, doesn't it?
Nonne saepenumeratum fit?

Do you think he *meant* to knock his block off?
Putasne eum caput illius removere in animo habuisse?

Q. **What's the score?**
A. **Lions 2 Christians 0**
Q. Quid est ratio?
A. Leones duo Christiani nihil

◆

Did you know the warm blood of a slaughtered gladiator will cure epilepsy?
Scibasne sanguinem calidum gladiatoris interfecti morbum comitialem sanare posse?

There are going to be 10,000 animals in the arena today.
Erunt decem milia animalium in arena hodie.

That Emperor's a bit bloodthirsty, isn't he?
Nonne ille Imperator paululum cruentum est?

Pooh! What a stink!
Fue! Odor horribilis!

I think he's *non compos mentis*.
Puto eum non compotem mentis esse.

Don't sit in the front row!
Noli sedere in ordine primo!

That's asking for it.
Illud provocat molestiam.

I like the women gladiators best.
Puto gladiatores femineas optimas esse.

Is the gladiator seeing visitors after the show?
Videtne gladiator salutatores post ludos?

**Not another tragedy! When is the
next comedy?**
*Non alia tragoedia! Quando est
comoedia proxima?*

Sit down! I can't see when you stand up.
Sede! Cum stas, tum non videre queo.

I bet he felt that.

Puto eum illud sentire.

◆

I can't look . . .

Non spectare queo . . .

◆

These seats aren't very comfortable, are they?

Num sedes commodissimum sunt?

◆

He doesn't stand a chance against that half-starved lion.

Contra leonem jejunem fortunam non habebit.

◆

I say, that's not done!
Edepol, non fas est!

◆

It was great fun last night. A thousand gladiators were killed.
Nox proxima oblectamentum magnum erat.
Mille gladiatores necati sunt.

◆

Who wants to join the Greens' fan club?
Qui sodalitatem viridum iungere cupit?

◆

No Reds allowed in this section.
Rubri in parte hac non permittuntur.

◆

Bet you ten silver coins he wins.
Pignore certo decem nummorum argenti victoriam eius futuram esse.

◆

AT THE
•BANQUET•

In wine is truth.

In vino veritas.

◆

I'm not sure I can manage another nine days of celebrations.

Non certus sum me posse ferre novem additos dies celebrationum.

◆

Not another speech!
Non oratio alia!

◆

I do like a nice bit of lamb's womb.
Dulce frustum uteri agni amo.

◆

Pass me that teat.
Da mihi illam papillam.

◆

That's a very flattering bust of you, old chap.
Non blandissima, amice mi, imago tui est.

◆

I'm going to take the rest home for breakfast.
Cetera domum ientaculo portabo.

Put some more pepper on my fruit.
Pone in fructu meo plus piperis.

◆

**He invited me to dinner to make me listen
to him recite his awful poems.**
*Me cenare vocavit ut me se poemas terribiles
recitantem audire cogeret.*

**I wish that dancer would keep
still; she's making me dizzy.**
*Cupio saltatricem quietam esse;
vertiginosum me facit.*

Are you drunk again?
Esne ebrius iterum?

◆

There's not enough fish sauce.
Non satis est liquaminis.

◆

What did the last food taster die of?
De quo praegustator proximus mortuus est?

◆

Fancy serving five-year-old wine!
Animo finge vinum quinquennium serviendum!

◆

Pass the port.
Da mihi vinum ex Oporto.

◆

Can I have a dormouse with that?
Gliremne cum illo habere possum?

◆

Can you show me the way to the vomitorium?
Demonstra mihi semitam ad vomitorium, sis?

◆

Not stuffed thrush again!
Non turdum saginatum iterum!

◆

How much for only half a feast?

Quantum pro epulae dimidium?

◆

I don't want rose petals in my wine.

Nolo habere rosas in vino meo.

◆

That painting is so faded I can't see what's for dinner.

Illa pictura est tam marcida ut non cibum cenae videre possim.

◆

Well, I've never eaten parrot before!

Numquam antehac psittacum sumpsi!

◆

Are those dormice fresh?

Suntne illi glires novi?

◆

Wash your hands before thanking the host.
Lava manus tuas antequam hospiti gratias agis.

◆

Put the rest of that boar in your serviette to bring home.
Pone cetera apri in linteo tuo domum ferre.

I do like a nice bit of duck.
Dulcem frustum anatis amo.

◆

What did you say liquamen is made of?
De quo dixisti liquamen fieri?

◆

**How many times have you been to
the vomitorium?**
Quot itinera ad vomitorium fecisti?

◆

Who invited you?
Quis te invitavit?

◆

No more boiled brains, thanks.
Non plus cerebrorum elixorum, gratias.

◆

I don't think I should've eaten that.
Non puto me illud edisse debere.

◆

Do you have any bigger bowls?
Habesne catinos maiores?

◆

Haven't you got any ostrich?
Nonne habes struthiocamelum?

◆

There's still a chicken claw in this.
Est unguis pulli in hoc.

◆

Can I be excused?
Excusarine me possum?

◆

That's the way I like it.
Illo modo id amo.

◆

I'm so sick of cabbage.
Sum tam fessus olere.

Let's look for his wine cellar.
Petamus cellam vinariam.

◆

No, I don't want goat's milk; that's for women.
Non desidero lac caprae; illud est mulieribus.

Haven't you got any more wine?
Nonnes habes plus vini?

This boar has a funny taste.
Hic aper gustum insuetum habet.

**I have to watch my figure –
only eight courses for me.**
*Necesse est mihi custodire figuram meam –
solum octo mensae mihi.*

What did you say this stuff was?
Quid dixisti hoc esse?

◆

**I must be a pleb at heart; I just can't
get used to lying down for dinner.**
*Vulgaris sum plebis in corde habeo; reclinare
cenae solere non possum.*

◆

**Do you have any elbow cushions? I was at a feast
last night and my elbow's still sore.**
*Habesne pulvinos cubito? Ad epulas nocte proxima veni et
cubitum adhuc est acerbum.*

◆

**I wish they'd throw some more rose petals
in the vomitorium.**
Desidero eos rosas plures in vomitorium iacturos esse.

◆

Are you sure these are oysters?
Esne certus eas esse ostreas?

Can we just have porridge tomorrow?
Iusne solum cras habere possumus?

No, I don't want syrup on my salmon.
Noli ponere defrutum in salmone meo.

**You managed all ten courses without one
visit to the vomitorium – well done, Claudius!**
*Edisti decem mensas sine aditu ad vomitorium –
benefactum, Claudi!*

Go to the vomitorium if you want to do that.
I ad vomitorium si illud facere cupis.

◆

I'm the chief guest.
Ego sum hospes primus.

◆

Do you mind not putting your elbow there?
Sis, noli ponere cubitum tuum illic.

◆

Do you think it would be very rude if I sat up?
Putasne id crudissimum futurum esse si sedeo?

◆

Ooh, eggs! My favourite!
O, ova! Deliciae meae!

Pass me one of those piglets, would you?
Da mihi unum illorum porcellorum, sis?

◆

**I wish I didn't have to share my couch
with him!**
Nolo dividere lectum meum cum eo!

Give the leftovers to the slaves.
Da servis tricas.

Wow – a fourteen-holder lamp stand!
Ecce! Candelabrum cum quattuordecim spatiis.

Oh no! We've arrived just in time to say prayers to the household gods.
Eheu! Tempore precum Laribus et Penatibus venimus.

I've found a hairpin in my soup.
In iure meo crinale inveni.

The music's a bit loud, isn't it?
Nonne musica strepentior est?

I think we'd better invite the neighbours in.
Puto nos finitimos invitare debere.

Why is Gaius wearing a pink toga?
Cur Gaius togam rubicundam gerit?

Keep the liquamen on hold.
Noli ferre liquamen.

◆

**What can I have if I don't like liquamen
or honey?**
*Quid habere possum si non liquamen aut
mel amo?*

◆

I drink, therefore I am.
Bibo, ergo sum.

◆

FINDING YOUR WAY AROUND
WAY AROUND
• THE MENU •

boiled must
caroenum

◆

thick fig syrup
defrutum

◆

very sweet wine sauce
passum

◆

pike livers
jecores luporum

◆

flamingo tongues
linguae phoenicopterorum

◆

peacock brains

cerebra pavonum

◆

pheasant brains

cerebra phasianorum

◆

hamburger

isicia omentata

◆

cooked watermelons and honeydew melons

pepones et melones

◆

fish with raisins

pisces cum astaphibus

◆

pear omelette
patina pirorum

◆

stuffed chicken
pullus fartus

◆

dates stewed with honey
palmulae cum melle

◆

egg sponge with milk
dulcia ex ovis et lacte

◆

boiled eggs
ova elixa

◆

stewed lamb
agnus coctus

◆

tuna with dates
thynni cum palmulis

◆

wine cakes
mustacei

◆

roast crane
grus assaria

◆

fried veal with raisins and honey
vitellina fricta cum acinis passis et melle

◆

soufflé topped with honey
tiropatinam

*salty fish sauce
liquamen

*fish goulash with liquamen
minutal marinum

*apricots hors d'oeuvres with liquamen
gustus armeniacorum cum liquamine

◆

*green beans with liquamen
fabaciae virides cum liquamine

◆

*chicken with liquamen
pullus cum liquamine

◆

*big shrimps and liquamen
scillae et liquamine

◆

*mussels with wine and liquamen
mituli cum vino et liquamine

◆

*boiled veal with honey and liquamen
vitellina elixa cum melle et liquamine

◆

*Recipe for liquamen: take some fish intestines and gills, fish juice and blood, add dried herbs such as coriander, oregano and mint, making a layer on the bottom of the container, then follow with a layer of fish, then a layer of salt two fingers high. Repeat these three layers until the container is filled. Let it rest for seven days in the sun. Then mix the sauce daily for twenty days. After that time it becomes a liquid.

◆ GIRL TALK ◆

Do you like my new scent?
Amasne odorem meum novum?

◆

Bring me the rat's-head mixture;
my hair is looking thin today.
Porta mihi misturam capitis muris;
coma mea tenuis hodie apparet.

◆

I need another face pack.
Egeo curiatione alia vultui meo.

Where did you put my false teeth?
Ubi dentes falsos meos posuisti?

◆

Your eyebrows need plucking, my dear.
Supercilia tua, cara mea, carpenda sunt.

◆

Do you have any sweets for bad breath?

Habesne dulcia pro halitu malo?

◆

The men are good-looking around here, aren't they?

Nonne viri hic pulcherrimi?

◆

I'd like to meet a nice charioteer tonight.

Hac nocte aurigam dulcem invenire spero.

◆

I feel another fainting fit coming on.

Langorem alium apparere sentio.

◆

Feed this baby again, would you?
Sivis, ale infantem iterum?

◆

Hold my pet monkey.
Tene simiam meam.

◆

You're wearing a tad too much rouge, my dear.
Plus parvo purpurissum, cara mea, geris.

◆

I need to get some more poison.
Egeo plus veneni.

◆

I want one just like hers.
Unum consimile eius cupio.

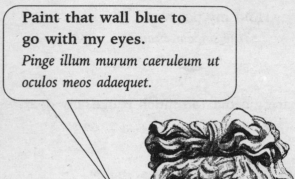

**Paint that wall blue to
go with my eyes.**
*Pinge illum murum caeruleum ut
oculos meos adaequet.*

**Please don't read any of your poetry out again at
dinner or we'll lose the rest of our friends.**
*Sis, noli legere poemas tuas iterum cena aut relictos
amicos amittemus.*

I have nothing to wear to the arena tonight.
Nihil gerere ad arenam hac nocte habeo.

◆

That toga is a bit tight on you, isn't it?
Nonne toga illa tibi minima paulo est?

◆

I really don't want to know how many people you killed today.
Non desidero scire quot hodie interfecisti.

◆

I need a good-looking slave to tend my plants.
Servo pulchro ut plantas meas curet egeo.

◆

Do hurry up and finish that mosaic.
Propera et fini illum tesellatum.

◆

This maintenance payment isn't nearly enough.
Hoc stipendium sustentationis non multo satis est.

◆

I hope you get better seats in the amphitheatre this time.
In amphitheatro hoc tempore sedes meliores te conducere spero.

◆

I'm leaving you; I find your behaviour irritating.
Te relinquo; mores tuos agitantes invenio.

◆

Why you had to promise a feast for the slaves is beyond me.
Cur epulas servis promittere cogereris non intellego.

◆

I need at least eight slaves to carry my litter.
Octo servis minime lectam portare egeo.

◆

I'm going to worship the household gods.
Ut Lares et Penates colam eo.

◆

**You will bring me a gold necklace back,
won't you, dear?**
Nonne torquem auri mihi, care, referes?

◆

**It is way too hot here; we must leave for the
country this week.**
*Est calidissimum hic; ad rurem hoc hebdomade
ire debemus.*

◆

Come and admire my roses.
Veni et mirari rosas meas.

◆

Have you seen my new fountain?
Fontemne novum meum vidisti?

◆

Oh, please don't write another poem.
Sivis, noli scribere poemam aliam.

◆

What do you mean 'marriage is a disagreeable burden'?
Quid significas 'matrimonium est onus molestum'?

◆

Take this child away; it's too noisy.
Remove hunc puerum; clamosissimus est.

◆

Braid my hair, and make it quick.
Intexe comam meam, et velociter.

◆

◆ SHOPPING ◆

I'd like to order twenty peacocks for my
banquet tomorrow and one hundred snails
gorged on milk.
*Viginti pavones et centum limaces satiatas lacte pro convivio
cras reservare cupio.*

◆

Can you make my toga shorter?
Potesne facere togam meam breviorem?

◆

Can I pay in beans?
Licetne mihi in fabis pendere?

I need a scribe to write a letter home for me.
Egeo scriba epistulam domum mihi scribere.

◆

We have much better shops than this in Rome.
Tabernas meliores multo quam has Romae habemus.

◆

Take this letter back to Rome for me.
Refer epistulam hanc Romam mihi.

◆

These prices are extortionate.
Pretia haec sunt altissima.

◆

I'd like a better magic potion than the one you gave him.

Desidero potionem magicam meliorem quam illam quam ei dedisti.

I'd like some new shoes; no, I don't need hobnails, I'm not a legionary.

Cupio calceos novos; non egeo clavis, legionarius non sum.

Have you got any good board games?
Habesne ludos tabulae ullos bonos?

◆

Are you allowed to sell poison in this town?
Licetne tibi vendere venenum in hoc oppido?

◆

Let the buyer beware.
Caveat emptor.

◆

**Oh no! Mother is going to be another
hour shopping.**
Eheu! Mater horam aliam in emptione aget.

◆

I didn't buy a thing all day.
Nullum hodie emi.

◆

Do you have it in a bigger size?
Habesne unum maius?

◆

You can pick up some great bargains if you look hard enough.
Empta optime invenies si caute spectas.

◆

That bread looks a bit stale.
Panis ille effetus apparet.

◆

I need some souvenirs to take home.
Memorandis domus portare egeo.

◆

How much for the ox?
Quot nummi pro bove cupis?

◆

Are those dates fresh?
Suntne palmulae novae?

I don't like the look of those sow's udders.
Speciem illorum uberum suis non amo.

When is the next shipment due?
Quando veniet congeries proxima?

I must buy some amber before it sells out.
Debeo emere sucinum antequam omne venditum est.

These trinkets are not cheap, are they?
Num hae tricae viles sunt?

Where can I find a dormouse breeder?
Ubi nutricem glirum invenire possum?

◆

I'd like an amphora of fish sauce.
Amphoram gari desidero.

Do you know where I can buy sow's udders in this town?
Scisne ubi in hoc oppido ubera suis emere possem?

◆ SETBACKS ◆

I've just been run over by a chariot.
Nuper ab biga transcursus sum.

◆

Help! I've fallen in the moat.
Iuva me! In fossam aquae cecidi.

◆

The crocodiles have got loose!
Crocidili liberi sunt!

◆

Where can I hire six bodyguards?
Ubi sex satelles conducere possum?

◆

I've been kicked by brats.
Calcitratus sum a pusionibus.

◆

**I can't get any sleep in this town; the shopkeepers
were moving wagons all night again.**
*In urbe non dormire possum; mercatores per totam noctem
carros movebant iterum.*

◆

**Watch out down there! I'm throwing the slops
out of the window.**
Vigila infra! E fenestra tricas iacturus sum.

◆

I think he put a curse on me!
Puto eum maledictum mihi dixisse!

◆

Those stupid firemen have put out my
barbecue again!
*Isti stulti pugnatores ignis fornacem foris
iterum exstinxerunt!*

◆

It's all your fault it happened; you put your left
shoe on first this morning.
Culpa tua est; hodie sinistram soleam primum induisti.

◆

I've just been drenched by a chamber pot.
Nuper ab olla camerae madefactus sum.

◆

No, you can't buy your freedom yet.
Nondum libertatem tuam comparare potes.

◆

Only a man could have planned this itinerary.
When am I supposed to go shopping?
Vir solus hoc consilium itineris facere potuit. Ubi tabernas
visitare potero?

◆

I've just fallen through my litter!
Nunc per lecticam cecidi!

◆

He dropped me!
Me demisit!

◆

Someone stepped on my toe!
Aliquis in digito pedis meo gressus est!

◆

I see why that dog is called Ferox!
Cerno cur canis iste Ferox vocetur!

◆

I knew I shouldn't have done that on an unlucky day.

Scivi me non fecisse debere id in die infelice.

By Hercules! I've banged my leg on that blessed bed frame again.

Mehercule! Crus meum in margine lecti iterum pulsavi.

Does anyone know the best cure for a hangover?
Scitne aliquis remedium optimum crapulae?

My wig's blown away again.
Iterum capillamentum meum flatum est.

Ow! I got a splinter where it hurts!
Uah! Fragmentum ligni ubi nocet habeo!

I spit in your face!
Sputo in tuum vultum!

I have a terrible hangover.
Crapulam terribilem habeo.

PERSONAL
•CARE•

Don't come near me with that scalpel!
Noli appropinquare me cum illo scalpello!

◆

Where did I put my false teeth?
Ubi dentes falsos meos posui?

◆

Your instrument is rather fearsome.
Instrumentum tuum tremendum est.

**You certainly have an impressive array
of instruments.**
Aciem gravem instrumentorum habes.

Do you have a catheter that will fit me?
Habesne catheterem qui mihi idoneus est?

**Do you have anything for inflammation of
the stomach?**
Aliquidne pro inflammatione stomachi habes?

Do you do enemas?
Facisne enemata?

◆

**Clean out my ear with that scoop,
would you?**
Purgesne aurem meam cum palula?

Do you think it's ringworm?
Putasne eum esse vermem anuli?

My finger needs strengthening with a
long-horn fingerstall.

Digitus meus cum fultera digiti cornus firmari eget.

◆

I have bladder pains here.

Dolores vesicae hic habeo.

◆

I hope you won't prescribe another sweat-bath.

Spero te non aliud balneum sudoris praescripturum esse.

◆

I need another operation on my rectum.

In recto meo aliam actionem chiurgi egeo.

◆

Get me the doctor; I think I need some leeches.

Voca medicum mihi; puto me hirudinibus egere.

◆

Smell my evacuations; I don't feel well.
Olface faeces meas; non valeo.

Do you have a remedy for bad breath?
Habesne remedium halitu malo?

What can I do about rotten teeth?
Quid de dentibus putridis facere possum?

Will it get better if I rub dried cow dung on it?
Melius erit si cum faece sicca vaccae id frico?

Can I make an appointment for blood-letting?
Pactumne hirudini facere possum?

**Do you have government health care
in this town?**
Habesne in hoc oppido medicinam municipalem?

◆

Oh no, I've run out of scurvy ointment.
Eheu, non habeo unguentum porrigini.

◆

This mustard gargle is disgusting!
Hoc gagarisma sinapis est foeda!

◆

They are my false teeth.
Sunt mei dentes falsi.

**Can I have some garlic in
milk for my asthma?**
*Possumne habere alium in
lacte pro anhelitu?*

Are you sure these potions are genuine?
Certus es has potiones esse veras?

◆

**That vinegar lotion has done wonders for
my runny eyes.**
Fluidum aceti pro oculis lacrimosis meis miracula faciebat.

◆

My ivory tooth's fallen out again.
Dens eboris meus iterum excidit.

◆

**My chilblains have flared up again.
I must get some hot turnips.**
Perniones mei iterum veniunt; egeo rapis calidis.

◆

WHAT TO SAY TO THE • CHILDREN •

Willing or not, you're going home now.
Volens nolens domum nunc is.

◆

To err is human.
Errare humanum est.

◆

I'll have you flogged.
Te flagellari esse iubebo.

◆

Yes, you *do* have to go to school.
Vere ad ludum incessurus es.

◆

**I'll send you to gladiator school like your brother,
and with any luck I'll never see you again.**
*Te ad ludum gladiatorum cum fratre tuo mittam,
et cum fortuna numquam iterum te videbo.*

◆

No, you can't bring your dog to London.
Canem tuum Londinium non ferre licet.

◆

**Thank the gods – only three more years till
you join the army.**
*Gratias deis – solum tres annos plures dum
te exercitui iungis.*

◆

No one goes to the toilet in the middle of the night.
Nemo ad latrinam in media nocte it.

◆

Don't throw stones at the gladiators.
Noli iacere saxa contra gladiatores.

◆

Leave some of that cake for the household gods.
Relinque partem placentae Laribus et Penatibus.

◆

No, you can't come to the feast.
Certe ad epulas non venire potes.

◆

Don't talk to him; he's a pleb.
Noli loqui ei; vulgaris est.

◆

No, you can't have another silver coin.
Alium nummum argenti habere non potes.

◆

The soothsayer said I should leave you at home.
Vates dixit me debere te domi relinquere.

Children should be seen and not heard.
Liberi visi et non auditi esse debent.

Don't be puerile.
Noli esse puerilis.

Be very nice to the tax-collector's son!
Filio exactoris tributorum benignus esto!

Here's another nut to play with, dear.
Hic est nux alia ludo, care.

Now take your nuts and get out of here.
Cape nuces tuas et amove.

I'll sell you if you don't behave.
Te vendam si non bene moratus es.

Shut up and sit down! [singular]
Sile et sede!

Shut up and sit down! [plural]
Silete et sedete!

You'll have to repeat a year at this rate.
Hoc modo annum repetere habebis.

Leave me in peace.
Relinque me in pace.

◆

Enough, already.
Satis, nunc.

◆

Don't come crying to me!
Noli venire mihi et lacrimare!

◆

Tidy your room, young man.
Purge cameram tuam, puer.

◆

No, you can't have a pet dormouse.
Non glirem delicias habere potes.

Go and watch that juggler while I nip off
to the toilets for half an hour.
*I et specta illum praestigiatorem dum ad latrinas
dimidium horae eo.*

It's not nice to pelt him with olive stones when he's asleep.
Non dulce est cum seminibus olivarum eum ferire dum dormit.

◆

Like father, like son.
Ut pater, sic filius.

◆

Don't those teachers teach you anything?
Nonne magistri illi ullum tibi docent?

◆

Be quiet!
Tace!

◆

VENI VIDI
•WHAT?•

I came, I saw, I cried.
Veni, vidi, vagii.

◆

I came, I saw, I fled.
Veni, vidi, verti.

◆

I came, I saw, I survived.
Veni, vidi, vixi.

◆

I came, I saw, I inspected.
Veni, vidi, visi.

◆

I came, I saw, I burned.
Veni, vidi, vaporavi.

I came, I saw, I wavered.
Veni, vidi, variavi.

◆

I came, I saw, I avoided.
Veni, vidi, vitavi.

◆

I came, I saw, I sold out.
Veni, vidi, vendidi.

◆

I came, I saw, I aged.
Veni, vidi, veteravi.

I came, I saw, I ate it all.
Veni, vidi, voravi.

◆

I came, I saw, I threw up.
Veni, vidi, vomui.

◆

I came, I saw, I got tougher.
Veni, vidi, valui.

◆

I came, I saw, I took a beating.
Veni, vidi, vapulavi.

◆

◆ MISCELLANEA ◆

I'm writing a guide book to these heathen lands.
It will make a lot of money for the publisher.
Scribo librum ad dirigendum per illas terras paganas.
Pecuniam magnam librario importabit.

◆

You Britons are very smelly.
Vos Britanni odoratissimi estis.

◆

You let women rule tribes?
Feminas regere nationes permittitis?

◆

Where's a centurion when you need one?
Ubi centurio est cum uno eges?

◆

When is the next chariot due?
Quando veniet currus proximus?

◆

**You wait an hour for a chariot to turn up
and then three arrive at once!**
*Unam horam dum currus veniat exspectas,
et tres simul veniunt!*

◆

Well, Rome wasn't built in a day.
Roma in una die non aedificata est.

◆

I want a new slave; you're useless . . .
Servum novum cupio; es inutilis . . .

◆

I wish we'd stayed at home!
Opto nos domi mansisse!

Call this a holiday?
Vocas hoc festum?

Out of my way. I am a Roman citizen.
Te refer e via mea. Civis Romanus sum.

◆

Gosh!
Edepol!

◆

Damn!
Di immortales!

◆

What this villa needs is a prison.
Haec villa carcere eget.

◆

The commuting is impossible around here.
Hic vir transcurrere non potest.

◆

That which you are doing does not please me.
Quod facitis me non iuvat.

◆

I pray that Titivilius may not lead me into very many errors.

Precor ne Titivilius me induxerit in permultos errores.

All Michael O'Mara titles are available by post from:

Bookpost, PO Box 29, Douglas, Isle of Man, IM99 1BQ

Credit cards accepted.
Telephone: 01624 677237
Fax: 01624 670923
Email: bookshop@enterprise.net
Internet: www.bookpost.co.uk

Free postage and packing in the UK.

Other Michael O'Mara Humour titles:

All Men Are Bastards – ISBN 1-85479-387-X pb £3.99
The Book of Urban Legends – ISBN 1-85479-932-0 pb £3.99
Born for the Job – ISBN 1-84317-099-X pb £5.99
The Complete Book of Farting – ISBN 1-85479-440-X pb £4.99
The Ultimate Book of Farting – ISBN 1-85479-596-1 hb £5.99
The Ultimate Insult – ISBN 1-85479-288-1 pb £5.99
Wicked Cockney Rhyming Slang – ISBN 1-85479-386-1 pb £3.99
Wicked Geordie English – ISBN 1-85479-342-X pb £3.99
Wicked Scouse English – ISBN 1-84317-006-X pb £3.99
The Wicked Wit of Jane Austen – ISBN 1-85479-652-6 hb £9.99
The Wicked Wit of Winston Churchill – ISBN 1-85479-529-5 hb £9.99
The Wicked Wit of Oscar Wilde – ISBN 1-85479-542-2 hb £9.99
The World's Stupidest Criminals – ISBN 1-85479-879-0 pb £3.99
The World's Stupidest Graffiti – ISBN 1-85479-876-6 pb £3.99
The World's Stupidest Laws – ISBN 1-85479-549-X pb £3.99
The World's Stupidest Men – ISBN 1-85479-508-2 pb £3.99
The World's Stupidest Signs – ISBN 1-85479-555-4 pb £3.99
More of the World's Stupidest Signs – ISBN 1-84317-032-9 pb £4.99
The World's Stupidest Last Words – ISBN 1-84317-021-3 pb £4.99
The World's Stupidest Inventions – ISBN 1-84317-036-1 pb £5.99
The World's Stupidest Instructions – ISBN 1-84317-078-7 pb £4.99
The World's Stupidest Sporting Screw-Ups – ISBN 1-84317-039-6 pb £4.99
Shite's Unoriginal Miscellany – ISBN 1-84317-064-7 hb £9.99
Cricket: It's A Funny Old Game – ISBN 1-84317-090-6 pb £4.99
Football: It's A Funny Old Game – ISBN 1-84317-091-4 pb £4.99